Irresistible Ultimate Crock Pot Cookbook for Beginners 2024

Carol Kelley

Table of contents

Chapter 4:beef

Beer Braised Beef

Collard Green Beef Sauté

Collard Green Beef Sauté

Spicy Taco-Worthy Beef Meat

BBQ Beef Brisket

Cowboy Beef

Vegetable Beef Roast with Horseradish

Beef Salsa Chili

Chapter 5:Pork

Apple Bourbon Pork Chops

Coconut Pork Delight

Mango Flavored Pulled Pork

Pork Sausage Stew

Curried Roasted Pork

Great Pork Carnitas

Delicious Pork Roast

Tomato Sauce Pork Roast

Chorizo Spicy Pork

Conclusion

Introduction

Welcome to the world of delicious, hassle-free cooking with the Crock Pot Cookbook! Imagine walking through your front door after a long, hectic day, and being greeted by the irresistible aroma of a homemade meal, just like Grandma used to make. With a few simple steps, you'll have dinner on the table in no time, allowing the whole family to indulge in a satisfying and nourishing meal together.

No need to be a master chef to create mouthwatering dishes in your own kitchen. The Crock Pot allows you to effortlessly whip up your favorite comfort foods without breaking a sweat. Each recipe in this cookbook is a celebration of flavor, offering a wide array of options that will satisfy your taste buds and nourish your body.

With this comprehensive slow cooker cookbook by your side, you'll never run out of new recipes to try. Whether you're short on time, lack confidence in the kitchen, or simply want to simplify your cooking routine, this cookbook has got you covered. Brace yourself for a chorus of "make-it-again" requests from your loved ones!

Discover the versatility of your crock pot as you explore a wide range of dishes. From delicious overnight breakfasts that cook while you sleep, to prepping ingredients in the morning for a warm, home-cooked meal at the end of the day, the possibilities are endless. Your crock pot will become your go-to kitchen tool for creating tantalizing meals and entertaining dishes.

So, get ready to dive into the world of easy and flavorful cooking with the Crock Pot Cookbook. Whether you're a busy professional, a novice cook, or simply looking to add convenience to your culinary repertoire, this cookbook will be your guide to creating memorable meals that will delight your taste buds and nourish your body. Let the crock pot revolutionize your kitchen experience and make cooking a joyous celebration!

Carol Kelley is committed to improving reader satisfaction,With the aim of enabling all readers to create delicious and abundant dishes using common ingredients, your review holds significant reference value for potential readers, helping them make informed purchasing decisions. We sincerely invite you to take a moment to leave your valuable feedback on the purchasing platform. Your support and recognition are of great significance to my writing career. You can contact us at laihongchun70@gmail.com to receive the latest updates of free chapter releases and exquisite gifts.

Chapter 1:Crock Pot Basics

Embark on a culinary journey as we delve into the fascinating world of Crock-Pot cooking. From its origins to its impact on modern kitchens, we explore the nuances that make this cooking method a game-changer. Get ready to enhance your culinary expertise and revolutionize your approach to home-cooked meals.

What is Crock-Pot?

Unlocking the Essence of Slow Cooking

Crock-Pot, a brand synonymous with slow cooking, has revolutionized the way we approach meal preparation. It's not just a kitchen appliance; it's a culinary ally that transforms simple ingredients into mouthwatering masterpieces over time. Let's explore the core aspects of what makes Crock-Pot an essential addition to your kitchen.

The History of Crock-Pot

Unraveling the Origins

In the 1970s, the Crock-Pot emerged as a household name, introducing the concept of slow cooking to busy families. Developed by Rival Industries, this innovative appliance aimed to simplify meal preparation, allowing individuals to enjoy home-cooked goodness without spending hours in the kitchen.

How Does Crock-Pot Work?

The Art of Slow and Steady

Crock-Pot operates on the principle of slow cooking, utilizing low temperatures over an extended period. This method ensures flavors meld harmoniously, and tougher cuts of meat tenderize, resulting in succulent dishes. The device's ability to simmer and stew gradually produces meals that are rich in taste and texture.

Tips for Crock-Pot Mastery

Elevating Your Culinary Skills

- **Layering Flavors:** Build complexity by layering ingredients strategically for a harmonious taste profile.

- **Appropriate Cuts:** Choose cuts of meat suitable for slow cooking, ensuring tenderness and flavor infusion.

- **Timing is Everything:** Master the art of timing to achieve the perfect balance of textures and tastes in your creations.

Advantages of Crock Pot Cooking

A Paradigm Shift in Cooking

- **Time Efficiency**: Crock-Pot allows for hands-off cooking, freeing up your schedule while flavors intensify.

- **Nutrient Retention**: Slow cooking preserves nutrients, ensuring your meals are not only delicious but also wholesome.

- **Versatility:** From soups to desserts, Crock-Pot accommodates a diverse range of recipes, offering unparalleled flexibility.

Here are a few highlights:

Slow Cookers help you resist the temptation of constantly ordering takeout. With the ability to effortlessly prepare a wide variety of meals, you'll always have delicious homemade food ready when you are without relying on takeout!

Slow Cookers are a year-round cooking solution! Their versatility allows you to enjoy both summer and winter dishes any time of the year. Say goodbye to seasonal restrictions!

The slow, low-temperature cooking process of Slow Cookers is ideal for tenderizing less expensive cuts of meat without sacrificing flavor.

Slow cooking extracts the full array of flavors from your ingredients, making it perfect for preparing an array of dishes such as soups, stews, and casseroles.

Cooking with a Crock Pot

At its core, the Slow Cooking process requires minimal effort. Simply prepare your ingredients, place them in the Slow Cooker, and cover with the provided glass lid. Set the timer and heat level, and let the magic happen while you go about your day. However, to ensure the best Slow Cooking experience with your crock pot, consider these tips:

Fill your Crock Pot between one-half to three-fourths of the way. Overfilling will impede proper cooking.

Keep in mind that food at the bottom cooks faster and becomes more tender. Place root vegetables at the bottom to make the most of this.

For thicker and more concentrated juices, add a touch of cornstarch 10-15 minutes before the end of the cooking time.

When cooking meats, opt for cheaper cuts as they work better with Slow Cookers due to their lower fat content and ability to tenderize during extended cooking times.

Follow layering instructions carefully when using multiple ingredients. As a general rule, place vegetables at the bottom and meat at the top.

If cooking on low heat, avoid lifting the lid too often as it will add 20 minutes to the overall cooking time. Check progress by spinning the lid to let condensation fall off instead of fully removing it.

Prior to adding ground meat to your Crock Pot, cook and drain it in a skillet to remove excess fat.

For more intense flavors, consider browning large cuts of meat before adding them to the Crock Pot.

With these tips, you'll make the most of your Crock Pot's capabilities and unlock a world of delicious, convenient cooking.

Chapter 2:Breakfast
Delicious Early Morning Pudding

Serving: 4
Prep Time: 10 minutes
Cooking Time: 4 hours

Ingredients:

- 2 large eggs
- 1 teaspoon cinnamon
- ¼ teaspoon nutmeg
- Pinch of salt
- ¼ inch fresh ginger, peeled and grated
- ½ cup coconut milk
- 1 large sweet potato, peeled and grated
- 1 large crisp apple, peeled and grated
- ½ cup dried coconut
- ¼ cup raisins halved
- Coconut oil as needed
- ¼ cup toasted pecans, toasted

Directions:

1. Take a bowl and beat in eggs, spices, ginger, coconut milk
2. Whisk well until combined
3. Stir in grated sweet potato, apple, dried coconut, raisins
4. Grease the inside of Crock Pot with coconut oil
5. Pour egg mixture into the cooker and place lid, cook on
6. LOW for 4 hours
7. Serve warm with a topping of pecans, enjoy!

The Perfect Frittata

Serving: 4
Prep Time: 15 minutes
Cooking Time: 2 hours

Ingredients:
- 4 mushrooms, sliced
- 1 cup fresh spinach
- 2 garlic cloves, diced
- Coconut oil as needed
- 6-8 whole eggs
- Salt and pepper to taste

Directions:
1. Prepare your vegetables accordingly
2. Coat Crock Pot with a small amount of coconut oil
3. Beat eggs and tip them into the cooker
4. Add remaining ingredients and stir
5. Place lid and cook on HIGH for 2 hours until eggs are set
6. Remove the inside pan and tip frittata into a plate
7. Serve and enjoy!

The Great CocoLoco Pear Delight

Serving: 4
Prep Time: 5 minutes
Cooking Time: 8 hours

Ingredients:
- 6 ripe pears, deseeded and chopped
- 3 cups coconut, shredded
- 1 and ½ cups coconut milk
- 1 cup fresh pineapple, chopped
- 2/3 cup coconut butter
- 2 tablespoons coconut oil
- ½ teaspoon cinnamon
- ¼ teaspoon nutmeg
- Pinch of salt

Directions:
1. Add all of the listed ingredients into your Crock Pot
2. Place lid and cook on LOW for 8 hours
3. Serve and enjoy!

Great Morning Chicken Salad

Serving: 4
Prep Time: 10 minutes
Cooking Time: 4 hours

Ingredients:
- 2 pound boneless and skinless chicken breast
- ½ small onion, diced
- 2 ribs celery, diced
- ½ cup chicken stock
- 1 and ½ cups whole30 mayo
- ½ cups pecans, chopped
- ¼ teaspoon salt
- ¼ teaspoon pepper
- Fresh Dill

Directions:
1. Add chicken, onion, celery, stock to your Crock Pot
2. Cook on LOW for 3-4 hours until thoroughly cooked
3. Shred the chicken using a fork
4. Add chicken to a serving bowl and add mayo, grapes, salt,
5. pepper, pecans, and dill
6. Serve and enjoy!

Cheesy Sausage and Potato Casserole

Serving: 4
Prep Time: 15 minutes
Cooking Time: 4-6 hours on LOW

Ingredients:

- - 1 lb sausage, cooked and crumbled
- - 4 cups frozen shredded hash browns
- - 1 cup cheddar cheese, shredded
- - ½ cup onion, diced
- - ½ cup green bell pepper, diced
- - 6 eggs
- - 1 cup milk
- - Salt and pepper to taste
- - Optional toppings: chopped green onions, salsa

Directions:

1. Cook the sausage in a skillet until browned and crumbled. Drain any excess fat.
2. In a large mixing bowl, combine cooked sausage, frozen shredded hash browns, cheddar cheese, diced onion, and diced green bell pepper. Mix well.
3. In a separate bowl, whisk together eggs, milk, salt, and pepper.
4. Pour the egg mixture over the sausage and potato mixture. Stir to combine.
5. Line the inside of your Crock Pot with parchment paper or spray with non-stick cooking spray.
6. Transfer the mixture to the Crock Pot, spreading it evenly.
7. Cover with the Crock Pot lid and cook on LOW for 4-6 hours or until the eggs are set and the potatoes are tender.
8. Serve hot and garnish with optional toppings such as chopped green onions or salsa, if desired.

Shakshuka Egg Delight

Serving: 3
Prep Time: 15 minutes
Cooking Time: 3 hours 15 minutes

Ingredients:
- ¼ cup extra virgin olive oil
- ½ onion, sliced thinly
- 3 cups tomatoes, diced
- 3 garlic cloves, sliced
- ½ teaspoon paprika
- ½ teaspoon cayenne pepper
- ¾ teaspoon cumin
- Bay leaf
- Salt and pepper to taste
- 4-6 large eggs
- Parsley, chopped
- 1 jalapeno, seeded and minced
- 1 cup carrots, diced

Directions:
1. Coat bottom of Crock Pot with olive oil, add veggies,
2. herbs, and spices
3. Stir
4. Place lid and cook on HIGH for 3 hours4. Crack eggs directly into the dish and cook for 10-15
5. minutes more until egg whites are opaque
6. Scoop out the dish in serving bowls and sprinkle parsley
7. Enjoy!

Apple Cinnamon Oatmeal

Serving: 4
Prep Time: 10 minutes
Cooking Time: 7-8 hours on LOW or 3-4 hours on HIGH

Ingredients:
- - 2 cups rolled oats
- - 4 cups water
- - 2 cups apple, peeled, cored, and diced
- - ¼ cup honey or maple syrup
- - 1 teaspoon cinnamon
- - ½ teaspoon vanilla extract
- - Pinch of salt
- - Optional toppings: chopped nuts, raisins, additional honey or maple syrup

Directions:
1. In the Crock Pot, combine rolled oats, water, diced apple, honey or maple syrup, cinnamon, vanilla extract, and salt. Stir well to evenly distribute the ingredients.
2. Cover the Crock Pot with its lid and cook on LOW for 7-8 hours or on HIGH for 3-4 hours.
3. Stir well before serving. If desired, add optional toppings such as chopped nuts, raisins, or an extra drizzle of honey or maple syrup.

Breakfast Burrito Casserole

Serving: 6
Prep Time: 15 minutes
Cooking Time: 5-6 hours on LOW or 3-4 hours on HIGH

Ingredients:
- - 8 large eggs
- - ¼ cup milk
- - 1 lb breakfast sausage, cooked and crumbled
- - 1½ cups shredded cheddar cheese
- - 1 green bell pepper, diced
- - ½ onion, diced
- - 6 large flour tortillas
- - Salt and pepper to taste
- - Optional toppings: salsa, sour cream, chopped fresh cilantro

Directions:
1. In a large bowl, whisk together eggs, milk, salt, and pepper.
2. In the Crock Pot, layer half of the crumbled sausage, shredded cheddar cheese, diced bell pepper, and diced onion.
3. Place three tortillas on top, overlapping as needed.
4. Pour half of the egg mixture evenly over the tortillas.
5. Repeat the layers with the remaining ingredients, ending with the remaining egg mixture.
6. Cover the Crock Pot with its lid and cook on LOW for 5-6 hours or on HIGH for 3-4 hours, or until the eggs are set and the tortillas are soft.
7. Serve hot, and if desired, top with salsa, sour cream, and chopped fresh cilantro.

Berry Quinoa Breakfast Bowl

Serving: 2
Prep Time: 10 minutes
Cooking Time: 2-3 hours on LOW or 1-2 hours on HIGH

Ingredients:

- - 1 cup cooked quinoa
- - 1 cup almond milk (or any milk of your choice)
- - 1 cup mixed berries (such as strawberries, blueberries, and raspberries)
- - 2 tablespoons honey or maple syrup
- - ¼ cup sliced almonds
- - Optional toppings: Greek yogurt, chia seeds, additional honey or maple syrup

Directions:

1. In the Crock Pot, combine cooked quinoa, almond milk, mixed berries, and honey or maple syrup. Stir well.
2. Cover the Crock Pot with its lid and cook on LOW for 2-3 hours or on HIGH for 1-2 hours.
3. Stir in sliced almonds before serving.
4. Serve hot in bowls, and if desired, top with Greek yogurt, chia seeds, and an additional drizzle of honey or maple syrup.

Breakfast Stuffed Peppers

Serving: 4
Prep Time: 20 minutes
Cooking Time: 6-8 hours on LOW or 4-5 hours on HIGH

Ingredients:
- - 4 large bell peppers, any color
- - 6 large eggs
- - ½ cup milk
- - 1 cup cooked bacon, crumbled
- - 1 cup shredded cheddar cheese
- - Salt and pepper to taste
- - Optional toppings: chopped fresh herbs, hot sauce

Directions:
1. Cut off the tops of the bell peppers and remove the seeds and membranes. Place the bell peppers upright in the Crock Pot.
2. In a bowl, whisk together eggs, milk, salt, and pepper.
3. Stir in crumbled bacon and shredded cheddar cheese.
4. Pour the egg mixture into the bell peppers, filling each pepper about three-fourths full.
5. Cover the Crock Pot with its lid and cook on LOW for 6-8 hours or on HIGH for 4-5 hours, or until the eggs are set and the peppers are tender.
6. Carefully remove the stuffed peppers from the Crock Pot using tongs.
7. Serve hot, and if desired, garnish with chopped fresh herbs or a drizzle of hot sauce.

Overnight French Toast Casserole

Servings: 6
Prep Time: 20 minutes (plus overnight chilling)
Cooking Time: 4-5 hours on LOW or 2-3 hours on HIGH

Ingredients:

- - 1 loaf of French bread, cut into 1-inch thick slices
- - 6 large eggs
- - 1 ½ cups milk
- - ½ cup heavy cream
- - ½ cup granulated sugar
- - 1 tablespoon vanilla extract
- - ½ teaspoon ground cinnamon
- - ¼ teaspoon ground nutmeg
- - ¼ teaspoon salt
- - Optional toppings: powdered sugar, maple syrup, fresh berries

Directions:

1. In a bowl, whisk together eggs, milk, heavy cream, granulated sugar, vanilla extract, ground cinnamon, ground nutmeg, and salt.
2. Arrange the sliced French bread in layers in the Crock Pot.
3. Pour the egg mixture evenly over the bread slices, making sure to soak each slice.
4. Gently press down on the bread to ensure it is fully soaked.
5. Cover the Crock Pot with its lid and refrigerate overnight or for a minimum of 6 hours.
6. Remove the Crock Pot from the refrigerator and let it sit at room temperature for about 30 minutes.
7. Cook on LOW for 4-5 hours or on HIGH for 2-3 hours, or until the French toast is firm in the center and golden brown on the edges.
8. Serve hot, dusted with powdered sugar and topped with maple syrup and fresh berries, if desired.

Chapter 3:Chicken

Balsamic Braised Chicken with Swiss Chard

Serving: 8
Prep Time: 15 minutes
Cooking Time: 8 hours

Ingredients:
- - 8 chicken thighs
- - 1 can (15 oz.) diced tomatoes
- - 1 bunch Swiss chard, shredded
- - 1 large onion, sliced
- - 4 garlic cloves, chopped
- - 1/4 cup balsamic vinegar
- - 2 bay leaves
- - 1 cup chicken stock
- - 2 tablespoons olive oil
- - 2 anchovy fillets
- - 1 teaspoon dried thyme
- - 1 teaspoon red pepper flakes
- - Salt and pepper to taste

Directions:
In a skillet, heat olive oil over medium heat. Add sliced onion and chopped garlic. Sauté for 2 minutes until softened.

1. Add chicken thighs, diced tomatoes, shredded Swiss chard, balsamic vinegar, bay leaves, chicken stock, anchovy fillets, dried thyme, and red pepper flakes to the skillet. Season with salt and pepper.
2. Transfer the mixture to your Crock Pot.
3. Cover the Crock Pot with its lid and cook on low settings for 8 hours, allowing the flavors to meld together and the chicken to become tender.
4. Serve the balsamic braised chicken with Swiss chard warm and fresh

Chicken Taco Filling

Servings: 8
Prep Time: 15 minutes
Cooking Time: 6 hours

Ingredients:
- - 4 chicken breasts, halved
- - 1 cup chicken stock
- - 1 tbsp. taco seasoning
- - 1/2 tsp. cumin powder
- - 1/2 tsp. celery seeds
- - 1/4 tsp. chili powder
- - Salt and pepper to taste

Directions:
1. Begin by placing the halved chicken breasts in your crock pot.
2. Pour the chicken stock over the chicken. This will help keep the chicken moist and flavorful as it cooks.
3. Sprinkle the taco seasoning, cumin powder, celery seeds, and chili powder over the chicken. These spices will give the chicken a rich, taco-flavored taste.
4. Season the mixture with salt and pepper according to your taste preferences.
5. Cover the crock pot with its lid and set it to cook on low settings for 6 hours. The slow cooking process allows the chicken to become tender and absorb all the flavors of the spices and stock.
6. Once the cooking time is complete, take the chicken out of the crock pot and shred it into fine threads. This can be done using two forks or a shredder.
7. Serve the shredded chicken in taco shells. You can complement this filling with your favorite taco toppings such as lettuce, cheese, sour cream, salsa, and guacamole.
8. Enjoy your homemade Chicken Taco Filling as a delicious and easy-to-make meal, perfect for a family dinner or a gathering with friends.

Red Wine Chicken and Mushroom Stew

Servings: 6
Prep Time: 30 minutes
Cooking Time: 6 hours

Ingredients:
- - 6 chicken thighs
- - 4 cups sliced mushrooms
- - 1 cup chicken stock
- - 1/2 cup red wine
- - 4 garlic cloves, minced
- - 1 large onion, chopped
- - 1 bay leaf
- - 1 thyme sprig
- - Salt and pepper to taste

Directions:
1. Begin by placing the chicken thighs at the bottom of your crock pot. If possible, arrange them in a single layer for even cooking.
2. Add the chopped onion and minced garlic on top of the chicken. These will add a savory depth to the stew.
3. Scatter the sliced mushrooms over the onion and garlic. The mushrooms will provide a rich, earthy flavor to the dish.
4. Pour the red wine and chicken stock into the crock pot. The wine will add a robust flavor, while the stock will help keep everything moist and tender.
5. Tuck in the bay leaf and thyme sprig among the ingredients. These herbs will infuse the stew with their aromatic flavors.
6. Season the mixture with salt and pepper according to your taste preferences.
7. Cover the crock pot with its lid and set it to cook on low settings for 6 hours. This slow cooking process allows the chicken to become tender and the flavors of the mushrooms, wine, and herbs to meld together.
8. After 6 hours, remove the bay leaf and thyme sprig. Stir the stew gently to combine the flavors.
9. Serve the Red Wine Chicken and Mushroom Stew warm. It pairs beautifully with crusty bread, mashed potatoes, or a simple side salad for a complete and satisfying meal.

Garlicky Butter Roasted Chicken

Servings: 8
Prep Time: 15 minutes
Cooking Time: 8 hours

Ingredients:
- - 1 whole chicken
- - 1/2 cup chicken stock
- - 2 tbsp. chopped parsley
- - 1/4 cup butter, softened
- - 1 tsp. dried sage
- - 6 garlic cloves, minced
- - Salt and pepper to taste

Directions:
1. Start by preparing the garlic butter mixture. In a bowl, combine the softened butter, minced garlic, chopped parsley, dried sage, and a pinch each of salt and pepper. Mix these ingredients until well combined.
2. Prepare your whole chicken by placing it on a clean working board. Carefully lift the skin away from the breast and thigh areas of the chicken, creating little pockets.
3. Take the garlic butter mixture and stuff it under the skin of the chicken, in the pockets you've created. Spread it as evenly as possible for consistent flavor.
4. Once the chicken is stuffed with the garlic butter mixture, place it in your crock pot.
5. Pour the chicken stock around the chicken in the crock pot. The stock will help to keep the chicken moist during the cooking process and add extra flavor.
6. Cover the crock pot with its lid and set it to cook on low settings for 8 hours. This slow cooking process will ensure the chicken is thoroughly cooked and infused with the garlic and herb flavors, becoming tender and juicy.
7. After 8 hours, your Garlicky Butter Roasted Chicken will be ready to serve. The chicken should be moist and flavorful, with a subtle hint of garlic and herbs.
8. Serve the chicken fresh and hot, accompanied by your favorite side dish, such as roasted vegetables, mashed potatoes, or a fresh salad. This dish is perfect for a comforting family meal or a special occasion.

Buffalo Chicken Drumsticks

Servings: 8
Prep Time: 15 minutes
Cooking Time: 7 hours

Ingredients:
- - 4-lbs. chicken drumsticks
- - 1 cup cream cheese
- - 2 tbsp. tomato sauce
- - 2 cups hot BBQ sauce
- - 1 tbsp. cider vinegar
- - 1 tsp. Worcestershire sauce
- - Salt and pepper to taste

Directions:
1. Begin by placing the chicken drumsticks in your crock pot. Make sure to arrange them so that they cook evenly.
2. In a separate bowl, combine the cream cheese, tomato sauce, hot BBQ sauce, cider vinegar, and Worcestershire sauce. Stir these ingredients together until they are well mixed. This will create a flavorful and spicy sauce for the chicken.
3. Pour the sauce mixture over the chicken drumsticks in the crock pot, ensuring that all the drumsticks are coated evenly.
4. Season the mixture with salt and pepper according to your taste preferences. This will help balance the flavors and add an additional depth to the dish.
5. Cover the crock pot with its lid and set it to cook on low settings for 7 hours. The slow cooking process will allow the chicken to become tender and absorb the flavors of the Buffalo sauce.
6. After 7 hours, the Buffalo Chicken Drumsticks will be ready to serve. They should be tender, flavorful, and coated in a rich, spicy sauce.
7. Serve the chicken warm and fresh. These drumsticks are perfect for a casual family dinner, game day, or a social gathering. They pair wonderfully with sides like celery sticks, carrot sticks, and blue cheese or ranch dressing for dipping.

Cider Braised Chicken

Serving: 8
Prep Time: 10 minutes
Cooking Time: 8 hours

Ingredients:
- - 1 whole chicken, cut into smaller pieces
- - 1 ½ cups apple cider
- - 1 teaspoon dried thyme
- - 1 teaspoon cumin powder
- - 1 teaspoon dried oregano
- - Salt and pepper to taste

Directions:
1. Season the chicken pieces with salt, dried thyme, cumin powder, and dried oregano.
2. Place the seasoned chicken in your Crock Pot.
3. Pour the apple cider over the chicken.
4. Cover the Crock Pot with its lid and cook on low settings for 8 hours, allowing the flavors to develop and the chicken to become tender.
5. Serve the cider braised chicken warm with your favorite side dish.

Cheesy Chicken

Serving: 2
Prep Time: 5 minutes
Cooking Time: 2 hours

Ingredients:
- - 2 chicken breasts
- - 1 cup cream of chicken soup
- - 1 cup grated Cheddar cheese
- - 1/4 teaspoon garlic powder
- - Salt and pepper to taste

Directions:
1. In your Crock Pot, combine the chicken breasts, cream of chicken soup, grated Cheddar cheese, and garlic powder.
2. Season with salt and pepper to taste.
3. Cover the Crock Pot with its lid and cook on high settings for 2 hours, allowing the chicken to cook through and the cheese to melt into a cheesy sauce.
4. Serve the cheesy chicken warm, spooning plenty of the cheesy sauce over the chicken.

Cordon Bleu Chicken

Serving: 4
Prep Time: 10 minutes
Cooking Time: 6 hours

Ingredients:
- - 4 chicken breasts, boneless and skinless
- - 4 slices Cheddar cheese
- - 4 thick slices ham
- - 1/2 cup vegetable stock
- - 1 teaspoon dried thyme
- - Salt and pepper to taste

Directions:
1. Season the chicken breasts with salt, pepper, and dried thyme.
2. Place the seasoned chicken breasts in your Crock Pot.
3. Top each chicken breast with a slice of ham and a slice of Cheddar cheese.
4. Pour the vegetable stock into the Crock Pot.
5. Cover the Crock Pot with its lid and cook on low settings for 6 hours, allowing the flavors to meld and the chicken to become tender.
6. Serve the Cordon Bleu Chicken warm and fresh.

Traditional Savory Chicken

Serving: 8
Prep Time: 10 minutes
Cooking Time: 4 hours

Ingredients:
- 2 pounds chicken breast, boneless
- ½ cup low sodium chicken broth
- 1 teaspoon garlic, minced
- ½ teaspoon pepper

Directions:
1. Season the chicken with pepper and minced garlic then place in a Crock Pot
2. Start pouring the chicken broth over the chicken and cover the Crock Pot with your lid
3. Set the Crock Pot to high
4. Cook for 4 hours
5. Or cook 8 hours on low
6. When the chicken is tender, remove the chicken out from the Crock Pot and then place it on a flat surface
7. Shred the chicken by using two forks and returns back to the Crock Pot
8. Mix well
9. Serve it with your favorite vegetables and enjoy

Mexican Chicken Stew

Servings: 8
Prep Time: 15 minutes
Cooking Time: 8 hours

Ingredients:

- - 4 chicken breasts, cubed
- - 1 can (15 oz.) black beans, drained
- - 1 can (15 oz.) diced tomatoes
- - 1 can (10 oz.) sweet corn, drained
- - 1 cup chicken stock
- - 1/2 cup cream cheese
- - 1/2 teaspoon chili powder
- - 1 cup red salsa
- - 1 teaspoon taco seasoning
- - Salt and pepper to taste

Directions:

1. In your Crock Pot, combine the cubed chicken breasts, diced tomatoes, red salsa, black beans, sweet corn, taco seasoning, chili powder, chicken stock, and cream cheese.
2. Season with salt and pepper to taste.
3. Cover the Crock Pot with its lid and cook on low settings for 8 hours, allowing the flavors to meld together and the chicken to become tender.
4. Stir the stew well before serving, ensuring that the cream cheese is evenly mixed.
5. Serve the Mexican Chicken Stew warm and fresh.

Cheesy Chicken Burrito Filling

Servings: 6
Prep Time: 15 minutes
Cooking Time: 6 hours

Ingredients:

- - 1 ½ lbs. ground chicken
- - 1 can (10 oz.) sweet corn, drained
- - 1 can (15 oz.) black beans, drained
- - 1 can (15 oz.) diced tomatoes
- - 1 ½ cups grated Cheddar
- - 2 cups chicken stock
- - 2 tablespoons canola oil
- - 1 cup brown rice
- - 1 teaspoon chili powder
- - Salt and pepper to taste

Directions:

1. In a skillet, heat the canola oil over medium heat. Add the ground chicken and cook for a few minutes, stirring often, until it's cooked through. Transfer the cooked chicken to your Crock Pot.
2. Add the sweet corn, black beans, diced tomatoes, grated Cheddar, chicken stock, brown rice, and chili powder to the Crock Pot.
3. Season with salt and pepper to taste.
4. Cover the Crock Pot with its lid and cook on low settings for 6 hours, allowing all the flavors to blend and the rice to cook.
5. Stir the mixture well to ensure the cheese is evenly distributed.
6. Serve the Cheesy Chicken Burrito Filling warm and fresh.

Coconut Ginger Chicken

Serving: 8

Prep Time: 15 minutes
Cooking Time: 7 hours

Ingredients:
- - 4 chicken breasts, halved
- - 1 lb. new potatoes
- - 1 lemongrass stalk, crushed
- - 4 garlic cloves, chopped
- - 2 teaspoons grated ginger
- - 1 shallot, chopped
- - 1 can baby corn, drained
- - 1 cup green peas
- - 1 ½ cups coconut milk
- - 1/2 cup green beans, chopped
- - 1/2 cup chicken stock
- - 1 bay leaf
- - Salt and pepper to taste
- - 2 tablespoons butter

Directions:
1. In a skillet, melt the butter over medium heat. Add the chicken breasts and cook for a few minutes on all sides until they are slightly browned. Transfer the chicken to your Crock Pot.
2. Add the new potatoes, crushed lemongrass stalk, chopped garlic cloves, grated ginger, chopped shallot, baby corn, green peas, coconut milk, green beans, chicken stock, bay leaf, salt, and pepper to the Crock Pot.
3. Adjust the taste with salt and pepper as needed.
4. Cover the Crock Pot with its lid and cook on low settings for 7 hours, allowing the flavors to meld together and the chicken to become tender.
5. Serve the Coconut Ginger Chicken warm.

Juicy Sweet Brown Chicken

Serving: 8

Prep Time: 15 minutes

Cooking Time: 3 and ½ hours

Ingredients:

- 2 pounds chicken, chopped
- 3 cups low sodium chicken broth
- ½ cup onion, chopped
- 2 teaspoons garlic, minced
- ¼ cup low sodium coconut aminos
- 1 teaspoon pepper
- Fresh celeries

Directions:

1. Place chopped chicken in the Crock Pot
2. Sprinkle sliced onion and minced garlic over the chicken then season with pepper
3. Drizzle coconut aminos over the chicken then using your hand rub till the chicken is fully seasoned
4. Pour chicken broth over the chicken covers the Crock Pot
5. Set the temperature to high
6. Cook for 3 and ½ hours
7. Once cooked, quick release the Crock Pot then take a serving dish and transfer the chicken and the liquid
8. Garnish with chopped celeries on top
9. Serve it warm and enjoy!

Chapter 4:beef

Corned Beef with Sauerkraut

Serving: 6

Prep Time: 15 minutes

Cooking Time: 8 hours

Ingredients:

- - 3 lbs. corned beef brisket
- - 1 lb. sauerkraut, shredded
- - 4 large carrots, sliced
- - 1 onion, sliced
- - 1 cup beef stock
- - 1/2 teaspoon cumin seeds
- - Salt and pepper to taste

Directions:

1. In your Crock Pot, combine the corned beef brisket, shredded sauerkraut, sliced carrots, sliced onion, beef stock, and cumin seeds.
2. Season with salt and pepper to taste.
3. Cover the Crock Pot with its lid and cook on low settings for 8 hours, allowing the flavors to meld together and the corned beef to become tender.
4. Once done, slice the corned beef and serve it warm, paired with the sauerkraut and vegetables.

Premium Ginger Beef

Serving: 4

Prep Time: 3 minutes

Cooking Time: 3-4 hours

Ingredients:

- 2 pounds cubed grass-fed beef roast
- 1 red bell pepper, chopped
- 1 cup sugar snap peas
- 3 garlic cloves, minced
- 3 carrots, sliced
- 2-4 tablespoons fresh ginger, grated
- 1 cup scallions, sliced
- 1 teaspoon red pepper flakes
- 2 tablespoons coconut aminos
- 2 tablespoons arrowroot powder
- 1 and ½ cups beef stock, organic
- Salt and pepper to taste

Directions:

1. Put all the ingredients except sugar snap peas in the Crock Pot
2. Set the Crock Pot to high
3. Cook for 3-4 hours
4. Once cooked, put the peas in a pot with a little water
5. Steam for 3 minutes until they turn bright green
6. Serve meat and peas with brown rice
7. Enjoy!

Old Fashioned Beef Stew

Serving: 6

Prep Time: 15 minutes

Cooking Time: 7 hours

Ingredients:

- - 1 ½ lbs. beef roast, cubed
- - 4 potatoes, peeled and cubed
- - 1 onion, chopped
- - 1 cup diced tomatoes
- - 1 ½ cups beef stock
- - 4 large carrots, sliced
- - 1 celery stalk, sliced
- - 2 tablespoons all-purpose flour
- - 2 parsnips, sliced
- - 2 tablespoons canola oil
- - 1 thyme sprig
- - 1 bay leaf
- - Salt and pepper to taste

Directions:

1. In a frying pan, heat the canola oil. Sprinkle the cubed beef roast with flour and place it in the hot oil. Fry on all sides until golden brown. Transfer the browned beef to your Crock Pot.
2. Add the diced tomatoes, beef stock, chopped onion, sliced carrots, sliced celery, cubed potatoes, sliced parsnips, thyme sprig, bay leaf, and season with salt and pepper to the Crock Pot.
3. Cover the Crock Pot with its lid and cook on low settings for 7 hours, allowing the flavors to meld together and the beef to become tender.
4. Stir the stew well before serving, ensuring the ingredients are evenly mixed.
5. Serve the Old Fashioned Beef Stew warm and fresh.

Jalapeno Braised Beef Flank Steaks

Servings: 4

Prep Time: 15 minutes

Cooking Time: 6 hours

Ingredients:

- - 4 jalapeno peppers, chopped
- - 4 flank steaks
- - 2 red bell peppers, cored and sliced
- - 1 can fire-roasted tomatoes
- - 1/2 tsp. cumin seeds
- - 1/2 tsp. mustard seeds
- - Salt and pepper to taste

Directions:

1. Prepare the jalapeno peppers by chopping them into small pieces. Remove the seeds and membranes if desired for less heat.
2. Place the flank steaks in the crock pot.
3. Add the chopped jalapeno peppers and sliced red bell peppers to the crock pot.
4. Pour in the fire-roasted tomatoes for a smoky flavor.
5. Sprinkle cumin seeds and mustard seeds over the ingredients.
6. Season with salt and pepper to taste.
7. Cook on low settings for 6 hours to ensure tender and flavorful steak.
8. Serve the Jalapeno Braised Beef Flank Steaks warm. Enjoy them as is or pair them with rice, salad, or tortillas for a complete meal.
9. This dish offers a perfect combination of spice and smokiness.

Cabbage Rice Beef Stew

Servings: 6

Prep Time: 30 minutes

Cooking Time: 6 hours

Ingredients:

- - 1-lb. beef roast, cut into thin strips
- - 1 head green cabbage, shredded
- - 2 ripe tomatoes, peeled and diced
- - 1 large onion, chopped
- - 1 large carrot, grated
- - 1 cup white rice
- - 1/4 cup water
- - 2 tbsp. tomato paste
- - 2 tbsp. canola oil
- - 1 cup beef stock
- - 1/2 tsp. chili powder
- - 1/2 tsp. cumin seeds
- - Salt and pepper to taste

Directions:

1. Heat canola oil in a frying pan over medium heat, then sauté the thin strips of beef roast until browned on all sides.
2. Transfer the browned beef to the crock pot.
3. Add shredded green cabbage, chopped onion, grated carrot, and diced tomatoes to the crock pot with the beef.
4. Stir in white rice, ensuring even distribution.
5. Pour beef stock and water into the crock pot for a rich stew.
6. Add tomato paste, cumin seeds, and chili powder for depth and heat.
7. Season with salt and pepper to taste.

8. Cook on low settings for 6 hours to ensure tender beef, cooked vegetables, and flavorful stew.
9. Stir thoroughly before serving the Cabbage Rice Beef Stew.
10. Serve warm, perfect for a comforting family meal.

Beer Braised Beef

Servings: 6

Prep Time: 15 minutes

Cooking Time: 8 hours

Ingredients:

- - 1/2-lb. baby carrots
- - 2 large potatoes, peeled and cubed
- - 1 cup dark beer
- - 2-lbs. beef sirloin
- - 1 large sweet onion, chopped
- - 4 garlic cloves, chopped
- - 1 sprig of thyme
- - 1/4 cup beef stock
- - 1 celery stalk, sliced
- - Salt and pepper to taste

Directions:

1. Prepare your vegetables by washing the baby carrots, peeling and cubing the potatoes, and chopping the sweet onion, garlic cloves, and celery.
2. Place the beef sirloin in the crock pot.
3. Add the prepared carrots, potatoes, onion, garlic, and celery to the crock pot.
4. Pour in the dark beer and beef stock for richness.
5. Add the thyme sprig for aromatic flavor.

6. Season with salt and pepper to taste.

7. Cook on low settings for 8 hours, allowing the flavors to meld together and the beef to become tender.

8. Serve the Beer Braised Beef warm, with the tender beef and flavorful vegetables.

9. Enjoy this hearty and delicious dish.

Collard Green Beef Sauté

Serving: 6

Prep Time: 15 minutes

Cooking Time: 3 hours

Ingredients:

- - 1 ½ lbs. beef roast, cut into thin strips
- - 2 bunches collard greens, shredded
- - 1/4 cup beef stock
- - 1/2 teaspoon cumin powder
- - 1 tablespoon all-purpose flour
- - 2 tablespoons canola oil
- - Salt and pepper to taste

Directions:

1. Season the beef strips with salt, pepper, flour, and cumin powder.
2. In a skillet, heat the canola oil over medium heat. Add the seasoned beef strips and cook for a few minutes, browning the beef on all sides. Transfer the browned beef to your Crock Pot.
3. Add the shredded collard greens and beef stock to the Crock Pot.
4. Cover the Crock Pot with its lid and cook on high settings for 3 hours, allowing the flavors to meld together and the beef to become tender.
5. Stir the sauté well before serving to ensure the ingredients are evenly mixed.
6. Serve the Collard Green Beef Sauté warm and fresh.

Collard Green Beef Sauté

Serving: 6

Prep Time: 15 minutes

Cooking Time: 3 hours

Ingredients:

- - 1 ½ lbs. beef roast, cut into thin strips
- - 2 bunches collard greens, shredded
- - 1/4 cup beef stock
- - 1/2 teaspoon cumin powder
- - 1 tablespoon all-purpose flour
- - 2 tablespoons canola oil
- - Salt and pepper to taste

Directions:

1. Season the beef strips with salt, pepper, flour, and cumin powder.
2. In a skillet, heat the canola oil over medium heat. Add the seasoned beef strips and cook for a few minutes, browning the beef on all sides. Transfer the browned beef to your Crock Pot.
3. Add the shredded collard greens and beef stock to the Crock Pot.
4. Cover the Crock Pot with its lid and cook on high settings for 3 hours, allowing the flavors to meld together and the beef to become tender.
5. Stir the sauté well before serving to ensure the ingredients are evenly mixed.
6. Serve the Collard Green Beef Sauté warm and fresh.

Spicy Taco-Worthy Beef Meat

Serving: 4

Prep Time: 12 minutes

Cooking Time: 4 hours

Ingredients:

- 2 pounds grass-fed ground beef
- ¼ teaspoon paprika
- ½ teaspoon onion powder
- ¼ teaspoon red pepper, crushed
- ½ teaspoon garlic powder
- 1 tablespoon chili powder
- ½ teaspoon oregano, dried
- 3 teaspoons tomato paste
- 1 teaspoon cumin

- 1 teaspoon sea salt

Directions:

1. Take a bowl and mix all the spices together
2. Add beef, spices and tomato paste into the Crock Pot and mix properly
3. Set the Crock Pot to low
4. Cook for 4 hours
5. Once cooked, make sure the meat is all broken apart before serving
6. Serve warm and enjoy!

Beef Okra Tomato Stew

Serving: 6

Prep Time: 15 minutes

Cooking Time: 6 hours

Ingredients:

- - 1 ½ lbs. beef roast, cut into thin strips
- - 1 can (15 oz.) diced tomatoes
- - 12 oz. frozen okra, chopped
- - 1 cup beef stock
- - 1 large onion, chopped
- - 4 garlic cloves, minced
- - 2 large potatoes, peeled and cubed
- - 1 thyme sprig
- - Salt and pepper to taste
- - Chopped parsley for serving

Directions:

1. In your Crock Pot, combine the beef roast, chopped onion, minced garlic cloves, diced tomatoes, chopped okra, cubed potatoes, beef stock, and thyme sprig.
2. Add salt and pepper to taste.
3. Cover the Crock Pot with its lid and cook on low settings for 6 hours, allowing the flavors to meld together and the beef to become tender.
4. Stir the stew well before serving, ensuring that all ingredients are evenly mixed.
5. Serve the Beef Okra Tomato Stew warm and fresh, or chilled if desired, and top with chopped parsley for added freshness and flavor.

BBQ Beef Brisket

Servings: 8

Prep Time: 15 minutes

Cooking Time: 6 hours

Ingredients:

- - 4 lbs. beef brisket
- - 1/4 cup apple cider vinegar
- - 1 cup ketchup
- - 1/2 cup beef stock
- - 1 tablespoon Worcestershire sauce
- - 2 tablespoons brown sugar
- - 2 tablespoons soy sauce
- - 1 teaspoon celery seeds
- - 1 teaspoon cumin powder
- - 1 teaspoon chili powder
- - 1 teaspoon smoked paprika
- - 1 teaspoon salt

Directions:

1. In a bowl, mix together the brown sugar, cumin powder, chili powder, celery seeds, smoked paprika, and salt.
2. Rub the spice mixture all over the beef brisket, ensuring it is evenly coated.
3. In your Crock Pot, combine the apple cider vinegar, beef stock, ketchup, Worcestershire sauce, and soy sauce.
4. Place the spice-rubbed brisket into the Crock Pot, ensuring it is immersed in the liquid mixture.
5. Cover the Crock Pot with its lid and cook on low settings for 6 hours, allowing the flavors to meld together and the beef to become tender.
6. Once done cooking, slice the beef brisket and serve it warm.

Cowboy Beef

Serving: 6

Prep Time: 15 minutes

Cooking Time: 6 hours

Ingredients:

- - 2 ½ lbs. beef sirloin roast
- - 1 can (15 oz.) red beans, drained
- - 6 bacon slices, chopped
- - 1 cup BBQ sauce
- - 2 onions, sliced
- - 1 teaspoon chili powder
- - 4 garlic cloves, chopped
- - Salt and pepper to taste
- - Coleslaw for serving

Directions:

1. In your Crock Pot, mix together the beef sirloin roast, chopped bacon, sliced onions, chopped garlic cloves, drained red beans, BBQ sauce, chili powder, salt, and pepper.
2. Cover the Crock Pot with its lid and cook on low settings for 6 hours, allowing the flavors to meld together and the beef to become tender.
3. Stir the mixture well before serving to ensure all ingredients are evenly mixed.
4. Serve the Cowboy Beef warm and fresh, and top with a portion of fresh coleslaw for added crunch and freshness.

Vegetable Beef Roast with Horseradish

Serving: 8

Prep Time: 15 minutes

Cooking Time: 6 hours

Ingredients:

- - 4 lbs. beef roast, trimmed of fat
- - 2 large carrots, sliced
- - 4 large potatoes, peeled and halved
- - 2 cups snap peas
- - 2 cups sliced mushrooms
- - 2 onions, quartered
- - 1 celery root, peeled and cubed
- - 1 cup beef stock
- - 1 cup water
- - Salt and pepper to taste
- - 1/4 cup prepared horseradish for serving

Directions:

1. In your Crock Pot, mix together the beef roast, sliced carrots, halved potatoes, snap peas, sliced mushrooms, quartered onions, and cubed celery root.
2. Pour in the beef stock and water.
3. Season with salt and pepper to taste.
4. Cover the Crock Pot with its lid and cook on low settings for 6 hours, allowing the flavors to meld together and the beef to become tender.
5. Once done, serve the Vegetable Beef Roast warm, with prepared horseradish as sauce on the side.

Beef Salsa Chili

Serving: 8

Prep Time: 15 minutes

Cooking Time: 7 hours

Ingredients:

- - 2 lbs. beef roast, cubed
- - 2 cups dried black beans
- - 2 garlic cloves, chopped
- - 2 red onions, chopped
- - 2 red bell peppers, cored and diced
- - 2 carrots, diced
- - 2 tablespoons canola oil
- - 4 cups chicken stock or water
- - 1 leek, sliced
- - 1 ½ cups red salsa
- - 1 teaspoon cumin seeds
- - 1 bay leaf
- - 1 teaspoon chili powder
  - Salt and pepper to taste

Directions:

1. In a skillet or frying pan, heat the canola oil. Add the cubed beef and cook for a few minutes until golden brown. Transfer the browned beef to your Crock Pot.
2. Add the dried black beans, chopped garlic cloves, chopped red onions, diced red bell peppers, diced carrots, sliced leek, red salsa, cumin seeds, bay leaf, chili powder, salt, and pepper to the Crock Pot.
3. Pour in the chicken stock or water.
4. Cover the Crock Pot with its lid and cook on low settings for 7 hours, allowing the flavors to meld together and the beef to become tender.
5. Stir the chili well before serving, ensuring all ingredients are evenly mixed.
6. Serve the Beef Salsa Chili warm.

Chapter 5:Pork

Apple Bourbon Pork Chops

Servings: 6

Prep Time: 10 minutes

Cooking Time: 8 hours

Ingredients:

- - 6 pork chops
- - 1/2 cup applesauce
- - 1/2 cup chicken stock
- - 1/4 cup bourbon
- - 1 sprig of rosemary
- - 1 sprig of thyme
- - 4 red apples, cored and sliced
- - Salt and pepper to taste

Directions:

1. Season the pork chops with salt and pepper.
2. In your Crock Pot, combine the apples, applesauce, chicken stock, bourbon, rosemary sprig, and thyme sprig.
3. Place the seasoned pork chops on top of the apple mixture in the Crock Pot.
4. Cover the Crock Pot with its lid and cook on low settings for 8 hours, allowing the flavors to meld together and the pork chops to become tender.
5. Remove the pork chops from the Crock Pot and serve them with the sauce found in the pot.

Coconut Pork Delight

Serving: 4

Prep Time: 10 minutes

Cooking Time: 4 Hours

Ingredients:

- 2 tablespoons coconut oil
- 4 pounds boneless pork shoulder, cut into 2-inch pieces
- Salt and pepper as need
- 1 large onion, chopped
- 3 tablespoons garlic cloves, minced
- 3 tablespoons fresh ginger, minced
- 1 tablespoon curry powder, mild
- 14 ounces tomatoes, diced
- 1 cup unsweetened coconut milk
- 2 cups chicken stock
- Green onions, chopped for garnish

Directions:

1. Take a large sized skillet and add coconut oil
2. Heat up and add pork in batches, brown them and season well with salt and pepper
3. Transfer to the Crock Pot
4. Add onion, ginger, garlic, cumin, turmeric, curry to the skillet (in fat from the pork) and cook for over low heat for 5 minutes
5. Transfer the mixture to Crock Pot and cook on LOW for 4 hours
6. Serve with a garnish of scallions and cilantro
7. Enjoy!

Mango Flavored Pulled Pork

Servings: 8

Prep Time: 15 minutes

Cooking Time: 7 hours

Ingredients:

- - 4-lbs. pork roast, cut into large pieces
- - 1 ripe mango, peeled and diced
- - 1 chipotle pepper, chopped
- - 1 cup BBQ sauce
- - 1/4 cup bourbon
- - 1 cup chicken stock
- - 1 tbsp. balsamic vinegar
- - Salt and pepper to taste

Directions:

1. Prepare the pork roast by cutting it into large pieces for even cooking and easier shredding later.
2. Dice the ripe mango to add a sweet and tropical flavor to the pulled pork.
3. Chop the chipotle pepper, being cautious with the spice level.
4. Place the pork pieces in the crock pot.
5. Add the diced mango and chopped chipotle pepper.
6. Pour in BBQ sauce, bourbon, and chicken stock for a flavorful sauce.
7. Drizzle with balsamic vinegar for tanginess.
8. Season with salt and pepper to taste.
9. Cook on low settings for 7 hours for tender and flavorful pork.
10. Shred the pork into fine threads using forks or a meat shredder.
11. Serve warm or chilled as preferred, perfect for sandwiches, tacos, or with rice and vegetables.

Pork Sausage Stew

Servings: 8

Prep Time: 15 minutes

Cooking Time: 6 hours

Ingredients:

- - 1-lb. fresh pork sausages, sliced
- - 2/3 cup brown lentils
- - 1 large onion, finely chopped
- - 1 cup red lentils
- - 2 carrots, diced
- - 2 garlic cloves, chopped
- - 1 celery stalk, diced
- - 1 bay leaf
- - 3 cups chicken stock
- - 1 cup diced tomatoes
- - 1 tbsp. tomato paste
- - 1 chipotle pepper, chopped
- - Salt and pepper to taste
- - 2 tbsp. chopped parsley for serving

Directions:

1. Prepare the ingredients by slicing the pork sausages, chopping the onion, carrot, garlic, and celery.
2. Place the sliced pork sausages in the crock pot.
3. Add the brown and red lentils.
4. Include the chopped onion, diced carrots, chopped garlic, and diced celery.
5. Pour in the diced tomatoes and tomato paste.
6. Add the chipotle pepper (adjust amount to taste).
7. Pour chicken stock over the ingredients.

8. Add the bay leaf (remove before serving).
9. Season with salt and pepper.
10. Cook on low settings for 6 hours.
11. Stir gently and remove the bay leaf.
12. Serve warm, garnished with chopped parsley.

Curried Roasted Pork

Servings: 6

Prep Time: 15 minutes

Cooking Time: 6 hours

Ingredients:

- - 2-lbs. pork roast
- - 1 cup coconut milk
- - 1 tsp. dried mint
- - 4 garlic cloves, minced
- - 1/2 tsp. chili powder
- - 1½ tsp. curry powder
- - 1 tsp. dried basil
- - Salt and pepper to taste

Directions:

1. Season the pork roast with a mixture of salt, pepper, curry powder, chili powder, minced garlic, dried mint, and dried basil. Rub the mixture all over the roast for even coating.
2. Place the seasoned pork in the crock pot.
3. Pour coconut milk over the pork to add creaminess and tenderness.
4. Cook on low settings for 6 hours to ensure tender pork infused with flavors.
5. Serve warm. It pairs well with steamed rice, salad, or roasted vegetables.
6. Enjoy this flavorful Curried Roasted Pork with its unique blend of spices and creamy coconut milk.

Brazilian Pork Stew

Serving: 6

Prep Time: 15 minutes

Cooking Time: 7 hours

Ingredients:

- - 1/2 lb. dried black beans
- - 1 ½ lbs. pork shoulder, cubed
- - 2 cups chicken stock
- - 2 sweet onions, chopped
- - 4 bacon slices, chopped
- - 4 garlic cloves, chopped
- - 2 bay leaves
- - 1 teaspoon cumin seeds
- - 1/2 teaspoon ground coriander
- - 1 teaspoon white wine vinegar
- - Salt and pepper to taste

Directions:

1. Rinse and sort the black beans, removing any debris. Place the black beans and cubed pork shoulder in your Crock Pot.
2. Add the chopped sweet onions, chopped bacon slices, chopped garlic cloves, bay leaves, cumin seeds, ground coriander, white wine vinegar, salt, and pepper to the Crock Pot.
3. Pour in the chicken stock.
4. Cover the Crock Pot with its lid and cook on low settings for 7 hours, allowing the flavors to meld together and the pork to become tender.
5. Stir the stew well before serving, ensuring all ingredients are evenly mixed.

Great Pork Carnitas

Serving: 8

Prep Time: 10 minutes

Cooking Time: 6 hours

Ingredients:

- 4 pounds boneless pork shoulder
- 1 tablespoon chili powder
- 1 teaspoon ground cumin
- 1 teaspoon salt
- ½ teaspoon pepper
- 1 tablespoon olive oil
- 2 limes, juiced
- 1 small onion, sliced
- 1 jalapeno, deseeded and sliced

Directions:

1. Rinse the pork shoulder carefully and pat them dry
2. Take a bowl and add chili powder, ground cumin, salt, pepper
3. Sprinkle the mixture all over the pork
4. Pat the meat with the dry rub
5. Transfer the meat to your Crock Pot and drizzle oil all over
6. Top with jalapeno, onion and squeeze lime juice
7. Place the lid and cook on LOW for 6 hours
8. Shred the meat with forks and remove any large sized fat chunks
9. Serve with a garnish of diced avocados and cilantro. Enjoy

Delicious Pork Roast

Serving: 6

Prep Time: 10 minutes

Cooking Time: 8 hours

Ingredients:

- 3 pounds pork shoulder roast, ethically raised
- 1 cup bone broth
- 6 sprigs fresh rosemary
- 4 sprigs fresh basil leaves
- 1 tablespoon chopped, chives
- ½ teaspoon salt
- ¼ teaspoon pepper, ground
- 3 apples, chopped

Directions:

1. Set your cooker to LOW and add the ingredients
2. Cook the apples over LOW settings for about 8-10 hours
3. Take out the cooked roast and carefully allow it to cool
4. Cut or shred it up into bite-sized portions and enjoy!

Tomato Sauce Pork Roast

Serving: 4

Prep Time: 5 minutes

Cooking Time: 3 hours

Ingredients:

- - 2 lbs. pork roast, cubed
- - 1/2 cup chicken stock
- - 1/2 cup tomato sauce
- - 2 tablespoons tomato paste
- - 2 tablespoons canola oil
- - 1/4 teaspoon cayenne pepper
- - Salt and pepper to taste

Directions:

1. In your Crock Pot, combine the cubed pork roast, chicken stock, tomato sauce, tomato paste, canola oil, and cayenne pepper.
2. Season with salt and pepper to taste.
3. Cover the Crock Pot with its lid and cook on high settings for 3 hours, allowing the flavors to meld together and the pork to become tender.
4. Stir the pork roast well before serving to ensure it is well-coated in the tomato sauce.
5. Serve the Tomato Sauce Pork Roast warm and fresh, paired with your favorite side dish.

Chorizo Spicy Pork

Serving: 3

Prep Time: 10 minutes

Cooking Time: 4 hours

Ingredients:

- 1 tablespoon paprika
- 1 teaspoon ancho chili powder
- 1 teaspoon salt
- 1 teaspoon ground cumin
- 1 teaspoon oregano
- ½ teaspoon pepper
- ¼ teaspoon cinnamon
- ¼ teaspoon coriander
- 2 pounds lean pork tenderloin
- 1 onion, diced
- 4 garlic cloves, minced
- 1 cup chicken broth
- 1 tablespoon apple vinegar

Directions:

1. Take a small sized bowl and add the spices
2. Rub the mixture over the pork
3. Transfer the pork to the Crock Pot and cover with onions
4. Add chicken broth and apple vinegar and cook on LOW for 4-6 hours
5. Shred the meat using a fork and serve with juices
6. If you want a crispier pork, just broil it for 2-3 minutes

Fennel Infused Pork Ham

Servings: 8

Prep Time: 15 minutes

Cooking Time: 6 hours

Ingredients:

- - 4-5 lbs. pork ham
- - 1/2 cup white wine
- - 2 fennel bulbs, sliced
- - 1 cup chicken stock
- - 1 thyme sprig
- - 2 bay leaves
- - 1 orange, zested and juiced
- - Salt and pepper to taste

Directions:

1. In your Crock Pot, combine the sliced fennel bulbs, orange zest, orange juice, white wine, chicken stock, thyme sprig, and bay leaves.
2. Season with salt and pepper to taste.
3. Place the pork ham on top of the fennel mixture in the Crock Pot.
4. Cover the Crock Pot with its lid and cook on low settings for 6 hours, allowing the flavors to meld together and the ham to become tender.
5. Remove the pork ham from the Crock Pot and slice it.
6. Serve the Fennel Infused Pork Ham warm.

Pineapple Cranberry Pork Ham

Servings: 6

Prep Time: 15 minutes

Cooking Time: 7 hours

Ingredients:

- - 2-3 lbs. smoked ham
- - 1 star anise
- - 1 bay leaf
- - 1 cup pineapple juice
- - 1 cup cranberry sauce
- - 1/2 teaspoon cumin powder
- - 1/2 teaspoon chili powder
- - 1 cinnamon stick
- - Salt and pepper to taste

Directions:

1. In your Crock Pot, mix together the cranberry sauce, pineapple juice, chili powder, cumin powder, cinnamon stick, star anise, and bay leaf.
2. Place the smoked ham in the Crock Pot and season with salt and pepper, if needed.
3. Cover the Crock Pot with its lid and cook on low settings for 7 hours, allowing the flavors to meld together and the ham to become tender.
4. Serve the Pineapple Cranberry Pork Ham warm with the sauce from the pot, paired with your favorite side dish.

Chapter 6:Ketogenic
Bacon and Spiced Egg Bake

Serving: 2

Prep Time: 10 minutes

Cooking Time: 1 hour

Ingredients:

- - 4 eggs
- - 4 slices streaky bacon
- - 1/2 teaspoon mixed spices (paprika, chili powder, cumin)
- - Fresh parsley, finely chopped
- - Olive oil for drizzling
- - Salt and pepper to taste

Directions:

1. Drizzle some olive oil into the Crock Pot to prevent sticking.
2. In a small bowl, lightly beat the eggs.
3. Add the mixed spices to the eggs along with a pinch of salt and pepper. Stir to combine.
4. Lay the bacon slices on the bottom of the Crock Pot.
5. Pour the spiced egg mixture over the bacon.
6. Place the lid onto the Crock Pot and set the temperature to LOW.
7. Cook for 1 hour or until the egg has set.
8. Heat some oil in a skillet or frying pan.
9. Carefully transfer the bacon and eggs as one piece to the pan and fry for 2 minutes until the bacon is crispy.
10. Serve the Bacon and Spiced Egg Bake on two plates, and sprinkle with fresh parsley for added flavor.

Chicken and Egg Soup

Serving: 6

Prep Time: 10 minutes

Cooking Time: 4 hours

Ingredients:

- - 4 chicken thighs, boneless and skinless, cut into medium-sized pieces
- - 4 garlic cloves, finely chopped
- - 1 red chili, finely chopped
- - 1 tablespoon finely grated fresh ginger
- - 1 lemon
- - 4 cups chicken stock
- - 6 eggs (1 egg per person)
- - Fresh coriander
- - Olive oil for drizzling
- - Salt and pepper to taste

Directions:

1. Drizzle some olive oil into the Crock Pot to prevent sticking.
2. Add the chicken thighs, chopped garlic cloves, chopped red chili, grated ginger, juice of one lemon, chicken stock, salt, and pepper to the Crock Pot. Stir to combine.
3. Place the lid onto the Crock Pot and set the temperature to HIGH.
4. Cook for 4 hours, allowing the flavors to meld together and the chicken to cook and become tender.
5. Remove the lid and stir the soup.
6. At this stage, there are two options:
   a. Option 1: Crack the eggs straight into the hot soup to lightly poach them.

   b. Option 2: Poach the eggs in a separate pot of water, and then place one poached egg into each serving bowl of soup.
7. Sprinkle each bowl of soup with fresh coriander for added flavor and freshness.

Chicken and Spinach Stew

Serving: 6-8

Prep Time: 10 minutes

Cooking Time: 8 hours

Ingredients:

- - 2 lb chicken thighs and legs, bone-in, skin-on
- - 2 cups spinach, roughly chopped
- - 1 onion, finely chopped
- - 6 garlic cloves, crushed
- - 1 teaspoon dried tarragon
- - 2 cups chicken stock
- - 1/2 cup dry white wine
- - 1/2 cup heavy cream
- - Olive oil for drizzling
- - Salt and pepper to taste

Directions:

1. Drizzle some olive oil into the Crock Pot to prevent sticking.
2. Add the chicken thighs and legs, chopped spinach, finely chopped onion, crushed garlic cloves, dried tarragon, chicken stock, salt, and pepper to the Crock Pot. Stir to combine.
3. Place the lid onto the Crock Pot and set the temperature to LOW.
4. Cook for 8 hours, allowing the flavors to meld together and the chicken to become tender.
5. In a small pot, drizzle some olive oil and add the remaining 2 cloves of crushed garlic.
6. Pour the dry white wine into the pot and simmer until it is reduced.
7. Stir in the heavy cream to the pot with the reduced wine and continue stirring to combine.
8. Remove the lid from the Crock Pot and stir the wine and cream mixture into the stew.
9. Serve the Chicken and Spinach Stew while hot.

Kale and Chicken Broth Soup

Serving: 4-6

Prep Time: 10 minutes

Cooking Time: 4 hours

Ingredients:

- - 6 garlic cloves, finely chopped
- - 3 tablespoons grated fresh ginger
- - 6 cups chicken stock
- - 1 large chicken breast, cut into small strips
- - 2 cups chopped fresh kale (stalks removed)
- - Olive oil for drizzling
- - Salt and pepper to taste

Directions:

1. Drizzle some olive oil into the Crock Pot to prevent sticking.
2. Add the finely chopped garlic, grated fresh ginger, chicken stock, small strips of chicken breast, chopped kale, salt, and pepper to the Crock Pot. Stir to combine.
3. Place the lid onto the Crock Pot and set the temperature to HIGH.
4. Cook for 4 hours, allowing the flavors to meld together and the chicken to cook through.
5. Serve the Kale and Chicken Broth Soup while steaming hot, adjusting the seasoning if necessary.

Crock Pot Beef Shank

Serving: 6

Prep Time: 15 minutes

Cooking Time: 8 hours

Ingredients:

- - 2 lb beef shanks
- - 1 onion, finely chopped
- - 5 garlic cloves, finely chopped
- - 2 cups red wine
- - 3 cups beef stock
- - Sprig of fresh rosemary
- - Olive oil for browning
- - Salt and pepper to taste

Directions:

1. Heat some olive oil in a skillet or frying pan and brown the beef shanks on all sides until sealed.
2. Remove the beef shanks from the skillet and set them aside.
3. Pour the red wine into the skillet and simmer to reduce the liquid.
4. Drizzle some olive oil into the Crock Pot to prevent sticking.
5. Add the browned beef shanks, finely chopped onion, finely chopped garlic cloves, reduced red wine, beef stock, sprig of fresh rosemary, salt, and pepper to the Crock Pot.
6. Secure the lid onto the Crock Pot and set the temperature to LOW.
7. Cook for 8 hours, allowing the beef shanks to become very tender.
8. Serve the Crock Pot Beef Shank while hot, accompanied by a side of vegetables for a complete meal

Stuffed Chicken Breasts

Serving: 4-6

Prep Time: 20 minutes

Cooking Time: 4 hours

Ingredients:

- - 4 large chicken breasts, skin off
- - 4 garlic cloves, finely chopped
- - 1/2 pound mozzarella cheese, sliced
- - 12 black olives, pit removed, chopped into chunks
- - 1 cup baby spinach, roughly chopped
- - 2 tomatoes, chopped
- - 1/2 teaspoon dried mixed herbs
- - 1/2 cup grated mozzarella cheese
- - Olive oil for rubbing
- - Salt and pepper to taste

Directions:

1. Slice each chicken breast lengthways, creating a cavity without slicing them into two separate pieces.
2. Rub the chicken breasts with olive oil and sprinkle with salt and pepper.
3. Stuff each chicken breast with the finely chopped garlic, sliced mozzarella cheese, chopped olives, and roughly chopped baby spinach.
4. Place the stuffed chicken breasts into the Crock Pot and pour the chopped tomatoes over the top. Sprinkle the dried mixed herbs over the tomatoes.
5. Set the temperature to HIGH.
6. Place the lid onto the Crock Pot and cook for 4 hours.
7. Sprinkle the grated mozzarella cheese over the top of the chicken breasts and place the lid back onto the Crock Pot. Continue cooking until the cheese has melted.
8. Serve the Stuffed Chicken Breasts while hot, and enjoy the melty, cheesy goodness!

Slow Cooked Savory Mince

Serving: 6-8

Prep Time: 10 minutes

Cooking Time: 8 hours

Ingredients:

- - 2 lb minced beef
- - 1 large onion, finely chopped
- - 4 garlic cloves, finely chopped
- - 2 celery stalks, finely chopped
- - 1 tablespoon butter
- - 3 cups beef stock
- - Olive oil for frying and drizzling
- - Salt and pepper to taste

Directions:

1. Heat some olive oil in a deep-sided frying pan.
2. Add the finely chopped celery, onion, and garlic to the pan and cook until they become soft and translucent.
3. Add the minced beef to the pan and cook for about 3 minutes to brown the meat.
4. Drizzle some olive oil into the Crock Pot to prevent sticking.
5. Transfer the cooked minced beef mixture to the Crock Pot.
6. Add the butter, beef stock, salt, and pepper to the Crock Pot and stir to combine all the ingredients.
7. Place the lid onto the Crock Pot and set the temperature to LOW.
8. Cook for 8 hours, allowing the flavors to meld together and the mince to become tender.
9. Serve the Slow Cooked Savory Mince while hot, and enjoy it with your preferred accompaniments.

Crock Pot Whole Chicken

Serving: Makes 1 whole chicken

Prep Time: 15 minutes

Cooking Time: 6 hours

Ingredients:

- - 1 medium-sized chicken
- - 1 teaspoon dried herbs (such as rosemary, thyme, or sage)
- - 1 lemon
- - 6 garlic cloves, skin kept on
- - 2 onions, cut into rough chunks
- - 3 celery sticks, cut into rough chunks
- - 3/4 cup chicken stock
- - 3 tablespoons butter
- - Olive oil for drizzling
- - Salt and pepper to taste

Directions:

1. Drizzle olive oil in the Crock Pot to prevent sticking.
2. Rub the whole chicken with olive oil, dried herbs, salt, and pepper.
3. Place the lemon inside the chicken cavity.
4. Add onions, celery, and garlic to the Crock Pot, pouring chicken stock over them.
5. Put the seasoned chicken on top of the vegetables.
6. Press a knob of butter onto the chicken's skin.
7. Set Crock Pot temperature to HIGH.
8. Cook for 6 hours until chicken is tender and fully cooked.
9. Remove the lid, let the chicken rest on a board to cool slightly before serving.
10. Use remaining liquid and vegetables to make gravy. Transfer to a pan, reduce, and adjust thickness with additional liquid or thickeners as needed.

Chapter 7: Vegetarian

Garlicky Lentil Stew

Serving: 6

Prep Time: 10 minutes

Cooking Time: 4 hours

Ingredients:

- - 1 cup red lentils
- - 6 garlic cloves, chopped
- - 1 onion, chopped
- - 1 cup vegetable stock
- - 1/2 teaspoon grated ginger
- - 1/2 teaspoon garam masala
- - 1 cup diced tomatoes
- - 1 cup coconut milk
- - 1 bay leaf
- - 1 sprig of thyme
- - 2 tablespoons tomato paste
- - 1 teaspoon brown sugar
- - Salt and pepper to taste

Directions:

1. In your Crock Pot, combine the red lentils, chopped garlic cloves, chopped onion, garam masala, grated ginger, diced tomatoes, coconut milk, vegetable stock, bay leaf, thyme sprig, tomato paste, brown sugar, salt, and pepper. Stir to combine all the ingredients.
2. Add salt and pepper to taste, adjusting the seasoning as desired.
3. Cook on low settings for 4 hours, allowing the lentils to become tender and the flavors to meld together.
4. Stir the Garlicky Lentil Stew well before serving to ensure all the ingredients are evenly mixed.
5. Serve the stew warm and fresh.

Slowly Cooked Tomato Salad

Serving: 4

Prep Time: 10 minutes

Cooking Time: 1 hour

Ingredients:

- 2 pounds tomatoes, core and cut into half
- 1 cup fresh basil leaves
- 2 tablespoons olive oil
- ½ onion, sliced
- Sea salt
- Pepper

Directions:

1. Add all ingredients into the Crock Pot and mix properly
2. Cover the lid
3. Set the Crock Pot to low
4. Cook for 1 hour
5. Serve and enjoy!

Tender Broccoli and Cauliflower Bites

Serving: 4

Prep Time: 10 minutes

Cooking Time: 2 hours

Ingredients:

- 1 pound broccoli florets
- 2 pounds baby carrots
- 1 tablespoon lemon juice
- 1 teaspoon cinnamon
- ½ cup unsweetened orange juice
- 2 tablespoons olive oil

Directions:

1. Add olive oil to brush inside of a Crock Pot
2. Then add broccoli florets and baby carrots into it
3. Drizzle the remaining lemon juice and olive oil then sprinkles cinnamon over the vegetables
4. Pour the orange juice into the Crock Pot
5. Set the Crock Pot to high
6. Cook for 2 hours
7. Once vegetables are cooked, open the lid
8. Take a serving dish and transfer the vegetables
9. You can take a preheated saucepan and sautés the vegetables for a few minutes
10. Serve it warm and enjoy!

Veggie Chickpea Curry

Serving: 6

Prep Time: 15 minutes

Cooking Time: 6 hours

Ingredients:

- - 1 cup dried chickpeas, rinsed
- - 2 potatoes, peeled and diced
- - 1 red bell pepper, cored and diced
- - 1 bay leaf
- - 2 garlic cloves, chopped
- - 1 carrot, sliced
- - 1 teaspoon curry powder
- - 1 Poblano pepper, chopped
- - 2 cups vegetable stock
- - 1 cup fire-roasted tomatoes
- - 1 large onion, chopped
- - 1 teaspoon grated ginger
- - Salt and pepper to taste
- - Chopped cilantro for serving

Directions:

1. In your Crock Pot, combine the rinsed chickpeas, diced potatoes, diced red bell pepper, bay leaf, chopped garlic cloves, sliced carrot, curry powder, chopped Poblano pepper, vegetable stock, fire-roasted tomatoes, chopped onion, grated ginger, salt, and pepper. Stir to combine all the ingredients.
2. Add salt and pepper to taste, adjusting the seasoning as desired.
3. Cook on low settings for 6 hours, allowing the flavors to meld together and the vegetables to become tender.
4. Stir the Veggie Chickpea Curry well before serving to ensure all the ingredients are evenly mixed.
5. Serve the curry warm, topped with chopped cilantro for added freshness and flavor.

Mesmerizing Kale Dish

Serving: 4

Prep Time: 10 minutes

Cooking Time: 3 hours

Ingredients:

- 2 pounds kale, chopped
- ¼ cup onion, chopped
- 2 teaspoons garlic, minced
- 1 cup low sodium chicken broth
- 2 tablespoons olive oil
- ½ teaspoon pepper

Directions:

1. Place chopped kale in a Crock Pot and press if it is required
2. Sprinkle garlic, onion, and pepper over the kale then add olive oil on top
3. Pour vegetable broth into the Crock Pot
4. Set the Crock Pot to high
5. Cook for 2 hours
6. Or cook 6 hours on low
7. Once kale is cooked take a serving dish and transfer the Kale
9. Serve it warm and enjoy!

Summer Squash Lasagna

Serving: 8

Prep Time: 20 minutes

Cooking Time: 6 hours and 30 minutes

Ingredients:

- - 2 summer squashes, cut into thin strips
- - 1 can chickpeas, drained
- - 1/2 cup red lentils
- - 1 shallot, chopped
- - 1 lemon, juiced
- - 1 1/2 cups shredded mozzarella
- - 4 tablespoons Italian pesto
- - 4 ripe tomatoes, pureed
- - 1/2 cup chopped parsley
- - 1 pinch chili flakes
- - 1/2 teaspoon dried thyme
- - Salt and pepper to taste

Directions:

1. In a bowl, mix together the drained chickpeas, red lentils, chopped parsley, lemon juice, dried thyme, and chili flakes. Add salt and pepper to taste and mix well to combine.
2. Place a few strips of summer squash in the Crock Pot. Brush the squash with pesto and top with a portion of the chickpea mixture. Spoon a few dollops of tomato puree over the layer.
3. Continue layering by adding more summer squash strips, pesto, chickpea mixture, and tomato puree.
4. Finish with a layer of shredded mozzarella on top.
5. Cook on low settings for 6 hours, allowing the flavors to meld together and the lasagna to become tender.

Strawberry and Asparagus Medley

Serving: 4

Prep Time: 12 minutes

Cooking Time: 3 hours

Ingredients:

- 2 pounds fresh asparagus
- 1 tablespoon ghee
- 1 cup low sodium vegetable broth
- ½ teaspoons garlic, minced
- 1 tablespoon olive oil

- ¾ cup fresh strawberry

Directions:

1. Cut the woody ends of the asparagus and then cut the asparagus into 2 inches of length
2. Use olive oil to brush inside of a Crock Pot then pour vegetable broth into it
3. Add ghee and garlic into the pot then stir well
4. Transfer the asparagus into the Crock Pot and cover it thoroughly
5. Set the Crock Pot to high
6. Cook for 3 hours
7. Or cook 6 hours on low
8. Once cooked, open the lid and take a serving dish and transfer the asparagus
9. Cut the fresh strawberries into quarters then garnish with strawberries on top
11. Serve and enjoy!

Sweet and Sour Red Cabbage Meal

Serving: 4

Prep Time: 12 minutes

Cooking Time: 2 hours

Ingredients:

- 4 cups red cabbage, chopped
- ½ cup parsley, chopped
- ¼ cup lemon juice
- 2 cups orange juice, unsweetened
- 1 tablespoon olive oil
- 1 teaspoon pepper
- 1 cup onion, chopped

Directions:

1. Pour olive oil into the Crock Pot then add red cabbage and onion into it
2. Add lemon juice and orange juice into the pot then season with pepper
3. Season with pepper
4. Cover the Crock Pot with the lid
5. Set the Crock Pot to high
6. Cook for 2 hours
7. Or cook 6 hours on low
8. Once cooked, open the lid and sprinkle with chopped parsley over the cabbage
9. Stir well
10. Take a serving dish and transfer the asparagus
11. Serve immediately and enjoy!

Quick Zucchini Stew

Serving: 4

Prep Time: 10 minutes

Cooking Time: 1 hour and 45 minutes

Ingredients:

- - 2 large zucchinis, cubed
- - 2 ripe tomatoes, diced
- - 1 shallot, chopped
- - 1 garlic clove, chopped
- - 1 bay leaf
- - 1/2 cup vegetable stock
- - 1 tablespoon olive oil
- - Salt and pepper to taste

Directions:

1. In your Crock Pot, combine the cubed zucchinis, diced tomatoes, chopped shallot, chopped garlic clove, bay leaf, vegetable stock, olive oil, salt, and pepper. Stir to combine all the ingredients.
2. Add salt and pepper to taste, adjusting the seasoning as desired.
3. Cook on high settings for 1 hour and 30 minutes, allowing the zucchini to become tender and the flavors to meld together.
4. Remove the bay leaf from the stew before serving.
5. Serve the Quick Zucchini Stew warm and fresh.

Bean Tomato Stew

Serving: 8

Prep Time: 15 minutes

Cooking Time: 7 hours and 30 minutes

Ingredients:

- - 2 red onions, chopped
- - 1 cup dried black beans, rinsed
- - 2 cups vegetable stock
- - 2 garlic cloves, chopped
- - 1 carrot, diced
- - 1 celery stalk, diced
- - 1 bay leaf
- - 1 red bell pepper, cored and diced
- - 2 tomatoes, peeled and diced
- - 1 cup water
- - 1 sprig of thyme
- - 1 cup fire-roasted tomatoes
- - 2 tablespoons tomato paste
- - Salt and pepper to taste

Directions:

1. In your Crock Pot, combine the chopped red onions, chopped garlic cloves, diced bell pepper, diced carrot, and diced celery. Stir to combine all the ingredients.
2. Add the rinsed black beans, vegetable stock, bay leaf, diced tomatoes, water, sprig of thyme, fire-roasted tomatoes, tomato paste, salt, and pepper to the Crock Pot. Stir to evenly distribute the ingredients and seasonings.
3. Cook on low settings for 7 hours, allowing the flavors to meld together and the beans to become tender.
4. Before serving, remove the bay leaf and thyme sprig from the stew.
5. Serve the Bean Tomato Stew warm.

Couscous with Vegetables

Serving: 6

Prep Time: 10 minutes

Cooking Time: 2 hours and 30 minutes

Ingredients:

- - 1/2 head of broccoli, cut into florets
- - 2 cups vegetable stock
- - 2 red bell peppers, cored and diced
- - 1 lemon, juiced
- - 1/2 cup chopped parsley
- - 1 cup couscous
- - 2 carrots, diced
- - 2 tablespoons chopped cilantro
- - Salt and pepper to taste

Directions:

1. In your Crock Pot, combine the couscous, vegetable stock, diced red bell peppers, diced carrots, and broccoli florets. Stir to combine all the ingredients.
2. Add salt and pepper to taste, adjusting the seasoning as desired.
3. Cook on high settings for 2 hours, allowing the vegetables to become tender and the couscous to cook through.
4. After cooking, stir in the lemon juice, chopped parsley, and chopped cilantro.
5. Serve the Couscous with Vegetables fresh.

Spicy Sweet Potato Chili

Serving: 8

Prep Time: 10 minutes

Cooking Time: 5 hours and 30 minutes

Ingredients:

- - 1 1/2 pounds sweet potatoes, peeled and cubed
- - 1 can (15 oz.) black beans, drained
- - 2 cups vegetable stock
- - 2 tablespoons tomato paste
- - 2 tablespoons olive oil
- - 2 shallots, chopped
- - 1 garlic clove, chopped
- - 1/4 teaspoon cumin powder
- - 1/2 teaspoon curry powder
- - 1 carrot, diced
- - 1/2 teaspoon chili powder
- - Salt and pepper to taste

Directions:

1. Heat the olive oil in a skillet and add the chopped shallots and garlic. Sauté for 2 minutes until fragrant, and then transfer the mixture to your Crock Pot.
2. Add the cubed sweet potatoes, drained black beans, vegetable stock, tomato paste, cumin powder, curry powder, diced carrot, chili powder, salt, and pepper to the Crock Pot. Stir to combine all ingredients.
3. Cook on low settings for 5 hours, allowing the flavors to meld together and the sweet potatoes to become tender.
4. Serve the Spicy Sweet Potato Chili warm.

Chapter 8: Seafood

Asparagus and Tilapia Packs

Serving: 4

Prep Time: 5 minutes

Cooking Time: 2 hours

Ingredients:

- 1 bundle asparagus
- 2 tablespoons ghee
- 4 tilapia fillets, thawed
- 8-12 tablespoons lemon juice
- Sprinkle of lemon pepper seasoning

Directions:

1. Cut a chunk of foil for every fillet and divide up the asparagus equally
2. With the fillet on the foil, season with lemon juice, lemon pepper seasoning, and ghee
3. Garnish with asparagus on top and fold over the foil, sealing the ends together
4. Set the Crock Pot to high
5. Cook for 2 hours
6. Once cooked, unwrap the packets carefully
7. Serve and enjoy

Great Spicy BBQ Shrimp

Serving: 4

Prep Time: 10 minutes

Cooking Time: 2 hours 45 minutes

Ingredients:

- 2 garlic cloves, minced
- 1 teaspoon Cajun seasoning
- ½ cup ghee
- ¼ cup Worcestershire sauce
- 1 tablespoon hot pepper sauce
- 1 lemon juice
- Salt and pepper to taste
- 1 and ½ pound large shrimp, unpeeled
- 1 green onion, chopped

Directions:

1. Add garlic, Cajun seasoning, ghee, sauce, hot pepper sauce, lemon juice to the crockpot
2. Season with salt and pepper and cover with lid
3. Cook on HIGH for 30 minutes
4. Rinse the shrimp properly and drain them
5. Spoon ½ of the sauce from the Crock Pot to a measuring cup
6. Add the shrimp to Crock Pot and drizzle sauce
7. Stir and coat well
8. Cover and cook on HIGH for 30 minutes until shrimp are opaque
8. Sprinkle with a bit of green onion and serve!

Two-Fish Soup

Servings: 8

Prep Time: 10 minutes

Cooking Time: 6 hours

Ingredients:

- - 1 sweet onion, chopped
- - 1 cup diced tomatoes
- - 1 lemon, juiced
- - 1 carrot, diced
- - 1 celery stalk, diced
- - 1 tbsp. canola oil
- - 3 cod fillets, cubed
- - 3 salmon fillets, cubed
- - 1 red bell pepper, cored and diced
- - 1 chipotle pepper, chopped
- - 2 tbsp. chopped parsley

- - Salt and pepper to taste

Directions:

1. Heat the canola oil in a skillet and sauté the chopped onion for 2 minutes until softened.
2. Transfer the sautéed onion to a crock pot. Add the diced tomatoes, lemon juice, diced carrot, diced celery, cubed cod fillets, cubed salmon fillets, diced red bell pepper, chopped chipotle pepper, and chopped parsley.
3. Season with salt and pepper to taste. Stir to combine all the ingredients.
4. Cook on low settings for 6 hours, allowing the flavors to blend and the fish to cook thoroughly.
5. Serve the Two-Fish Soup warm.

Fish Sweet Corn Soup

Servings: 6

Prep Time: 15 minutes

Cooking Time: 2 hours

Ingredients:

- - 1-lb. haddock fillets, cubed
- - 2 bacon slices, chopped
- - 1 sweet onion, chopped
- - 2 cups milk
- - 2 potatoes, peeled and diced
- - 2 cups frozen sweet corn
- - Salt and pepper to taste

Directions:

1. Cook the bacon in a skillet until crisp. Once done, transfer the cooked bacon to your crock pot.
2. To the crock pot, add the cubed haddock fillets, chopped sweet onion, diced potatoes, and frozen sweet corn.
3. Pour the milk over the ingredients in the crock pot.
4. Season with salt and pepper to taste.
5. Set your crock pot to cook on high settings for 2 hours. This cooking time allows the flavors to blend well and ensures that the fish and potatoes are cooked through.
6. Once finished, serve the Fish Sweet Corn Soup warm, ideally with crusty bread or a side salad.

Crazy Asian Salmon Fry

Serving: 4

Prep Time: 5 minutes

Cooking Time: 2-3 hours

Ingredients:

- 10-ounces salmon fillets
- 2 tablespoons coconut aminos
- 12-ounces Asian stir-fry vegetable blend, frozen
- 2 tablespoons lemon juice
- 2 tablespoons honey
- Salt and pepper to taste

Directions:

1. Remove the sauce packet from the vegetables
2. Pour vegetables into the Crock Pot
3. Season salmon with pepper and salt
4. Put on top of the vegetables
5. Mix soy sauce, lemon juice, and honey in a bowl
6. Pour over the veggies and salmon
7. Then close the Crock Pot lid
8. Set the Crock Pot to low
9. Cook for 2-3 hours
10. Serve fish with cooking liquid and with brown rice
11. Enjoy!

Hypnotic Salmon Curry

Serving: 4

Prep Time: 10 minutes

Cooking Time: 2 hours 45 minutes

Ingredients:

- 6 skinless tilapia fillets
- 1 onion, chopped
- 6 garlic cloves, chopped
- 2 teaspoons ginger, grated
- 3 stalks celery, chopped
- 2 carrots, chopped
- 2 cans coconut milk
- ½ cup vegetable stock
- 1 can tomato paste
- 1 and ½ teaspoons coriander
- 1 and ½ teaspoons cumin
- 1 teaspoon chili powder
- 2 teaspoons paprika
- 1 teaspoon turmeric
- ½ teaspoon pepper and ½ teaspoon salt
- Chopped cilantro, parsley, chili flakes for garnish

Directions:

1. Add 2 cans of coconut milk to the Crock Pot
2. Dollop tomato paste
3. Add vegetable stock, coriander, cumin, paprika, turmeric
4. Season with salt and pepper

5. Stir in the remaining ingredients
6. Place salmon pieces into the Crock Pot and add onion,
garlic, carrots, celery, and ginger
7. Place lid and cook on LOW for 2 hours and 4 minutes
8. Garnish and serve!

Salmon Fennel Soup

Servings: 6

Prep Time: 15 minutes

Cooking Time: 5 hours

Ingredients:

- - 3 salmon fillets, cubed
- - 1 lemon, juiced
- - 1 bay leaf
- - 1 fennel bulb, sliced
- - 1 carrot, diced
- - 1 shallot, chopped
- - 1 garlic clove, sliced
- - 1 celery stalk, sliced
- - Salt and pepper to taste

Directions:

1. In your crock pot, combine the chopped shallot, sliced garlic, sliced fennel bulb, diced carrot, and sliced celery.
2. Add the cubed salmon fillets to the mixture in the crock pot.
3. Pour the lemon juice over the ingredients and add a bay leaf for flavor.
4. Season the mixture with salt and pepper according to your taste preferences.
5. Set your crock pot to cook on low settings for 5 hours. This slow cooking process allows the flavors to meld beautifully and ensures the salmon is cooked perfectly.
6. Once the cooking time is complete, serve the Salmon Fennel Soup warm. This dish pairs well with crusty bread or a light salad.

The Orange and Mandarin Tilapia

Serving: 4

Prep Time: 5 minutes

Cooking Time: 2 hours

Ingredients:

- 4 tilapia filets
- 2 teaspoons garlic powder
- One 10-ounce can mandarin oranges, drained
- 2 tablespoons ghee, melted
- Salt and pepper to taste

Directions:

1. Lay out a piece of aluminum foil, it has to be large enough to fit all four fish fillets
2. Let them lay down side by side in the center of the foil and pour on ghee
3. Sprinkle garlic powder on fish evenly
4. Take a handful of oranges and lay them on each fillet
5. Finish off with a sprinkle of pepper and salt
6. Fold over the foil and seal the edges
7. Create a fish packet
8. Put in the Crock Pot
9. Set the Crock Pot to high
10. Cook for 2 hours
11. Remove the packet carefully
12. Serve and enjoy

Tomato Fish Soup

Servings: 6

Prep Time: 30 minutes

Cooking Time: 3 hours

Ingredients:

- - 1-lb. salmon fillets, cubed
- - 2 haddock fillets, cubed
- - 1 shallot, chopped
- - 4 ripe tomatoes, pureed
- - 2 cups vegetable stock
- - 2 garlic cloves, chopped
- - 1 tbsp. olive oil
- - 1 cup water
- - 1 bay leaf
- - 1 lemon, juiced
- - Salt and pepper to taste

Directions:

1. Heat the olive oil in a skillet. Add the chopped shallot and garlic and sauté for 2 minutes until they are softened.
2. Transfer the sautéed shallot and garlic into your crock pot.
3. Stir in the pureed tomatoes, vegetable stock, water, bay leaf, and lemon juice to the crock pot.
4. Season the mixture with salt and pepper to taste.
5. Set your crock pot to cook on high settings for 1 hour. This initial cooking time allows the flavors of the tomato base to develop.
6. After 1 hour, add the cubed salmon and haddock fillets to the crock pot.
7. Continue cooking for an additional 2 hours on high settings. This will ensure the fish is cooked through and absorbs the flavors of the soup.
8. Once done, the Tomato Fish Soup can be served warm or allowed to cool and served chilled, depending on your preference.

Chapter 9:Dessert

Spicy Chai Pears

Serving: 4

Prep Time: 5 minutes

Cooking Time: 3-4 hours

Ingredients:

- 5 whole cardamom pods
- 2 cups fresh orange juice
- 4 bosc pears
- 1 cinnamon stick, halved
- 1-inch piece ginger, sliced and peeled
- ¼ cup pure maple syrup

Directions:

1. Peel pears and cut off the bottom so that it stands up in the cooker
2. Remove the cores carefully without destroying the fruit
3. Put pears in the cooker, standing up
4. Add the rest of the ingredients, spooning some juice over the top of the pears
5. Set the Crock Pot to low
6. Cook for 3-4 hours, basting again with liquid every hour
7. When the pears are soft, they are ready to serve
8. Serve and enjoy!

Autumnal Bread Pudding

Servings: 8

Prep Time: 30 minutes

Cooking Time: 5 hours

Ingredients:

- - 16 oz. bread cubes
- - 1/2 cup golden raisins
- - 1/4 cup butter, melted
- - 2 red apples, peeled and diced
- - 2 pears, peeled and diced
- - 2 cups whole milk
- - 4 eggs, beaten
- - 1/2 cup white sugar
- - 1 tsp. vanilla extract
- - 1/2 tsp. cinnamon powder

Directions:

1. In your crock pot, mix together the bread cubes, diced apples, diced pears, and golden raisins.
2. In a separate bowl, combine the melted butter, whole milk, beaten eggs, white sugar, vanilla extract, and cinnamon powder. Whisk these ingredients together until well combined.
3. Pour this liquid mixture over the bread mixture in the crock pot, ensuring that the bread is evenly coated.
4. Cover the crock pot with its lid.
5. Set your crock pot to cook on low settings for 5 hours. This slow cooking process allows the bread to absorb the liquid mixture and the flavors to meld together, creating a soft and flavorful pudding.
6. Once the cooking time is complete, serve the Autumnal Bread Pudding slightly warm.

The Faux Banana Bread

Serving: 6

Prep Time: 5 minutes

Cooking Time: 3-4 hours

Ingredients:

- 1 tablespoon ghee
- 1 cup dates, pitted and mashed
- 3 large extra ripe banana, peeled and mashed
- 2 cups almond or coconut flour
- ¼ teaspoon nutmeg, grated
- 1 teaspoon cinnamon, ground
- 1 orange, zested
- 4 eggs, beaten

Directions:

1. Use ghee to grease the Crock Pot
2. Prepare all other ingredients as in the list above and blend together until the mixture has a smooth, even, creamy consistency
3. Pour into the Crock Pot
4. Cover the lid
5. Set the Crock Pot to low
6. Cook for 3-4 hours or until the bread is firm
7. Take a plate and slice the bread
8. Serve and enjoy!

The Great Lemon Pudding Cake

Serving: 4

Prep Time: 16 minutes

Cooking Time: 2 hours

Ingredients:

- 2 egg whites
- 2 egg yolks
- ¼ teaspoon salt
- 1 lemon's worth of juice and zest
- ¼ cup flour
- ½ cup coconut sugar
- Water

Directions:

1. Grease four 6-ounce ramekins
2. Take a bowl, whisk flour, salt and sugar in it
3. Mix egg yolks, lemon juice, lemon zest in another bowl
4. When smooth, add dry ingredients into wet until mixed properly
5. Beat the egg white until stiff peaks in another bowl
6. Fold whites into the batter
7. Divide batter into the ramekins and set the Crock Pot
8. Pour in just enough water to reach the halfway mark
9. Close the lid and set the Crock Pot to low
10. Cook for 2 hours
11. Cool for 10 minutes
12. Serve and enjoy

Cranberry Stuffed Apples

Servings: 4

Prep Time: 15 minutes

Cooking Time: 4 hours

Ingredients:

- - 4 large Granny Smith apples
- - 2 tbsp. honey
- - 1/4 cup ground almonds
- - 1/4 cup pecans, chopped
- - 1/2 cup dried cranberries
- - 1/2 cup apple cider
- - 1/4 tsp. cinnamon powder

Directions:

1. Begin by carefully removing the core from each Granny Smith apple. Ensure to create a hollow center large enough for the stuffing, but leave the bottom of the apples intact.
2. In a mixing bowl, combine the dried cranberries, honey, ground almonds, chopped pecans, and cinnamon powder. Stir these ingredients until they are well mixed.
3. Stuff each hollowed-out apple with this cranberry mixture, packing it gently.
4. Place the stuffed apples in your crock pot.
5. Pour the apple cider into the crock pot, around the apples. The cider will create a fragrant and flavorful base as the apples cook.
6. Cover the crock pot with its lid and set it to cook on low settings for 4 hours. This slow cooking process allows the apples to become tender and the flavors of the stuffing to infuse into the apples.
7. Once the cooking time is complete, the Cranberry Stuffed Apples are best served warm. They make a delicious and aromatic dessert, perfect for autumnal evenings or as a special treat.

Cocoa-Roasted Almonds

Serving: 4

Prep Time: 30 minutes

Cooking Time: 1 hour

Ingredients:

- 2 cups whole almonds
- 1 tablespoon organic cocoa powder
- Dash of salt
- 2 tablespoons ghee
- 1/3 cup organic coconut sugar
- 1 tablespoon pure vanilla extract

Directions:

1. Mix vanilla, nuts, sugar, salt, and cocoa in your Crock Pot, with ghee on top
2. Close the lid
3. Set the Crock Pot to high
4. Cook for 1 hour
5. Once cooked, open the lid then stir it and close the lid again
6. Cook for another 30 minutes on high
7. Stir and spread out on a wax paper-covered cookies sheet to cool
9. Serve and enjoy!

Lemon Berry Cake

Servings: 10

Prep Time: 30 minutes

Cooking Time: 4 hours

Ingredients:

- - 1 cup white sugar
- - 4 eggs
- - 1 cup all-purpose flour
- - 1 tsp. vanilla extract
- - 1 cup butter, softened
- - 1 cup fresh mixed berries
- - 2 tsp. lemon zest
- - 1 tsp. baking powder
- - 1/4 tsp. salt

Directions:

1. In a mixing bowl, combine the softened butter, white sugar, and vanilla extract. Beat them together until the mixture becomes creamy.
2. Add the eggs to the mixture, one at a time, mixing well after each addition. Then add the lemon zest and mix the ingredients at high speed for about 1 minute.
3. Gently fold in the all-purpose flour, baking powder, and salt into the mixture. Be careful not to overmix to ensure the cake remains light and fluffy.
4. Spoon the cake batter into your crock pot. Try to spread it evenly.
5. Sprinkle the fresh mixed berries on top of the batter. The berries will partially sink into the batter as it cooks.
6. Cover the crock pot with its lid and set it to cook on low settings for 4 hours. This slow cooking process allows the cake to bake gently, infusing the lemon and berry flavors throughout.
7. Once the cooking time is complete, turn off the crock pot and allow the Lemon Berry Cake to cool before serving.

Heart Throb Green Casserole

Serving: 6

Prep Time: 15 minutes

Cooking Time: 5 hours

Ingredients:

- 1 pound green beans
- 6 ounces fresh mushrooms
- 1 can (fat-free) cream of mushroom soup
- 1 teaspoon coconut aminos
- 1/8 teaspoon ground black pepper
- 1 cup French fried onions

Directions:

1. Spray your cooker with cooking spray
2. Wash the beans and trim them carefully
3. Cut the beans into even length and add them to your crockpot
4. Clean the mushrooms with a damp cloth and trim the stems
5. Cut them into slices and add to the cooker
6. Add aminos, ½ a cup of onion and black pepper
7. Stir well
8. Cover it up and cook for 4-6 hours
9. Remove the cover and add ½ a cup of the onion
10. Allow it to stay for 10 minutes (uncovered)
11. Once done, enjoy

Banana Chunk Cake

Servings: 10

Prep Time: 15 minutes

Cooking Time: 3 hours

Ingredients:

- - 1/2 cup butter, softened
- - 1/2 cup dark chocolate chips
- - 1/2 cup brown sugar
- - 1/4 cup milk
- - 1 cup all-purpose flour
- - 2 ripe bananas, sliced
- - 1/4 cup white sugar
- - 2 eggs
- - 2 tbsp. dark rum
- - 1 tsp. baking powder
- - 1/2 tsp. salt

Directions:

1. In a mixing bowl, cream together the softened butter, brown sugar, and white sugar. Beat them for a few minutes until the mixture becomes light and creamy.
2. Add the eggs to the bowl, one at a time, mixing well after each addition. Pour in the dark rum and milk, and give it a quick mix to incorporate.
3. Gently fold in the all-purpose flour, baking powder, and salt into the creamy mixture. Be careful to mix just until combined to keep the cake tender.
4. Stir in the sliced bananas and dark chocolate chips, distributing them evenly throughout the batter.
5. Grease the inside of your crock pot to prevent sticking, then pour the cake batter into it. Spread the batter evenly.

6. Cover the crock pot and set it to cook on high settings for 3 hours. This will bake the cake thoroughly and infuse the flavors of banana and chocolate.
7. Once the cooking time is up, turn off the crock pot and let the Banana Chunk Cake cool down. This cake is best served chilled, perhaps with a dollop of whipped cream or a drizzle of chocolate sauce for an extra treat.

Sweet Ginger Potatoes

Serving: 8

Prep Time: 10 minutes

Cooking Time: 3-4 hours

Ingredients:

- 2 and ½ pounds sweet potatoes
- 1 cup water
- 1 tablespoon fresh ginger
- ½ teaspoon ginger, minced
- ½ tablespoon ghee

Directions:

1. Peel the potatoes and quarter them
2. Add them to the Crock Pot
3. Add water, fresh ginger and ginger
4. Stir well
5. Cook on HIGH for 3-4 hours until the potatoes are tender
6. Add ghee and mash them
7. Serve immediately and enjoy

Strawberry Fudgy Brownies

Servings: 8

Prep Time: 15 minutes

Cooking Time: 2 hours

Ingredients:

- - 1/2 cup butter, cubed
- - 1/2 cup all-purpose flour
- - 1/2 cup applesauce
- - 1/4 cup cocoa powder
- - 1 cup dark chocolate chips
- - 1/2 cup white sugar
- - 2 eggs
- - 1 pinch salt
- - 1½ cups fresh strawberries, halved

Directions:

1. Mix cubed butter and dark chocolate chips in a heatproof bowl. Melt them together using a double boiler setup.
2. Remove from heat and stir in eggs, white sugar, and applesauce.
3. Gently fold in cocoa powder, all-purpose flour, and a pinch of salt until just combined.
4. Grease the crock pot and pour in the brownie batter, spreading it evenly.
5. Top with halved fresh strawberries.
6. Cook on high settings for 2 hours, allowing strawberries to soften and release some juice.
7. Let the Strawberry Fudgy Brownies cool before cutting into squares.
8. Serve as a delightful dessert, perfect with ice cream or whipped cream. Enjoy!

Maple Roasted Pears

Servings: 4

Prep Time: 15 minutes

Cooking Time: 6 hours

Ingredients:

- - 4 ripe pears, carefully peeled and cored
- - 1 cinnamon stick
- - 1/4 cup white wine
- - 2 cardamom pods, crushed
- - 1/4 cup maple syrup
- - 1/2 cup water
- - 1 tsp. grated ginger

Directions:

1. Prepare the pears by peeling and coring them while keeping the shape intact.
2. Place the pears in the crock pot.
3. Add cinnamon stick and crushed cardamom pods for aromatic flavor.
4. Pour in white wine and maple syrup to coat the pears with a rich syrup.
5. Add water for moisture.
6. Sprinkle grated ginger over the pears for a fresh, spicy kick.
7. Cook on low settings for 6 hours, allowing the pears to become tender and absorb the flavors.
8. Let the Maple Roasted Pears cool before serving as a sophisticated dessert, optionally with whipped cream or vanilla ice cream. Enjoy the delightful flavors!

Conclusion

As we reach the end of this culinary journey through the pages of our Crock Pot Cookbook, it's clear that the humble slow cooker is more than just a convenient kitchen appliance; it's a versatile tool that unlocks a world of flavors, textures, and comforting meals.

Throughout this book, we've explored an array of recipes that showcase the ease and versatility of slow cooking. From hearty soups and stews that simmer to perfection, to tender meats and delectable desserts, the Crock Pot proves itself as an indispensable ally in the kitchen. Each recipe, whether it's the savory depths of the Two-Fish Soup, the rich and comforting Autumnal Bread Pudding, or the delightfully sweet Maple Roasted Pears, is a testament to the fact that great cooking doesn't have to be complicated or time-consuming.

One of the most beautiful aspects of slow cooking is its ability to bring out complex flavors with minimal effort. This method of cooking allows ingredients to meld together over hours, creating layers of taste and aroma that can't be achieved in a hurry. It's also a way of cooking that encourages experimentation and adaptation. As we've seen in the recipes presented, ingredients can often be swapped, and new flavors can be introduced, making each dish uniquely yours.

Moreover, the Crock Pot is a solution for busy lifestyles, offering the luxury of home-cooked meals with the freedom of not having to stand over a stove. It's about coming home to a meal that's ready to be savored, a reminder of the simple joys of good food.

In conclusion, this cookbook is not just a collection of recipes; it's an invitation to embrace slow cooking as a way to enrich your culinary experience. The Crock Pot, with its simple settings and dependable results, is more than just a kitchen gadget—it's a pathway to creating nourishing, flavorful meals that bring people together. So, as you continue your culinary adventures, remember that great cooking is at your fingertips with the turn of a dial, proving that sometimes, the best things in life are those that require a little patience and a lot of love.

Made in the USA
Las Vegas, NV
10 January 2024

84162403R00077